TO _____

FROM _____

The ESSENCE OF
LEADERSHIP

MAC ANDERSON
BY THE FOUNDER OF *Successories®*

COUNTRYMAN

Nashville, Tennessee

table of contents

LEADERSHIP

A true leader has the confidence to stand alone, the courage to make tough decisions and the compassion to listen to the needs of others. They are much like eagles . . . They don't flock, you find them one at a time.

LEADERSHIP is a complicated topic, because there are probably as many definitions of leadership as there are leaders in the world. That's because a leader is a person with many roles . . . CEO, soldier, coach, entrepreneur, department head, politician, teacher, minister . . . as well as parent, spouse, and other personal roles. History has identified many qualities and characteristics of great leaders, and, of course, no person embodies them all. But the great leaders I've known, or read about, have one simple thing in common: They have developed their leadership styles around their personalities and their values, and in the end, their actions are consistent with what they truly believe.

Some people think leaders are born. I don't. I think leadership skills can be honed if we understand our strengths and weaknesses, and this understanding starts by knowing what to look for.

That's what this book is about. I've tried to capture the essence of leadership by sharing the most important lessons I've learned along the way. I've been very fortunate in meeting and working with many great leaders in my thirty years as an entrepreneur, and I've always loved reading biographies of entrepreneurs and other great leaders. Their insights about choices they made, their values, their commitment to hiring the best people, their passion for serving their customers, their courage, their ability to overcome adversity . . . these all made lasting impressions on me. As in my previous books, I've chosen in each chapter to make a point and reinforce it with a story. I find that the right story at the right time can inspire an "aha!" moment that bypasses the brain and goes right to the heart.

As a leader, it is my hope that this little book will be an inspiration to help you:

- Walk the talk,
- Keep it simple and keep it real,
- Celebrate successes,
- Know that courage matters,
- Keep hope alive,
- Take responsibility,
- Develop a "service attitude,"
- Aim for the heart, and . . .
- Make a difference whenever and wherever you can.

SERVICE

SERVICE IS THE LIFEBLOOD OF ANY ORGANIZATION.

EVERYTHING FLOWS FROM IT, AND IS NOURISHED BY IT.

CUSTOMER SERVICE IS NOT A DEPARTMENT.   IT'S AN ATTITUDE.

Learn from
SOUTHWEST AIRLINES

SOUTHWEST AIRLINES was founded in 1974 by Herb Kelleher with the simple goal of focusing on two things: hiring the best people and offering the best prices. His start–up airline has become legendary in the airline industry. Thirty years later, the market value of Southwest Airlines is now worth more than the next five airlines combined. I fly Southwest occasionally, and when someone mentions the name, I immediately think of enthusiastic employees who make work fun . . . fun for their customers, and fun for themselves. Of course, I'm not suggesting that having fun is the only reason for their success. They've made many other right decisions along the way. However, by building a culture around having fun and respecting one another, they have been able to attract great people who love serving their customers.

Not long also, I flew Southwest and the flight attendant announced, "I'm pleased to say we have a 99–year–old gentleman on board today. He's celebrating his birthday and this is the first time he's ever flown." Well, as you might imagine a light round of applause broke out. Then she said, "On the way out stop by the cockpit and wish him happy birthday." The cabin exploded with laughter.

Dan Zadra, the president of Compendium, is a friend of mine. He has his own theory about Southwest that came straight from Sheila, a flight attendant who he met on a trip from Seattle to Phoenix. Dan watched Sheila move with boundless energy to calm a crying child, plump an old man's pillow, trade jokes with the passengers, and answer questions in English, Spanish, and Japanese.

At one point, Sheila spilled an apron full of pretzels in the aisle, and Dan instinctively moved to help her. She said, "That's okay, Dan, it's my turn." Dan then said, "How did you know my name, and what do you mean it's your turn? I haven't done anything yet."

A good name, like goodwill, is got by many actions and lost by one.

LORD JEFFERY

Sheila smiled and answered, "I saw your name when I took your ticket. I always try to remember my passengers' names. It's polite. And taking turns is something I live by. I believe we all take turns serving each other in life. Right now, it's my turn to serve you, and I want you to really enjoy yourself on my flight. Someday, you may have the chance to serve me or my daughter or my dad. And when it's your turn I'm sure you'll do a great job."

Success doesn't happen by accident. It starts with an unwavering commitment from the leaders to build a dedicated team of passionate people who serve their boss . . . THE CUSTOMER.

VISION

WE ARE THE MUSIC MAKERS,
WE ARE THE DREAMERS OF DREAMS . . .

WE ARE THE MOVERS AND SHAKERS
OF THE WORLD FOR EVER, IT SEEMS.

ARTHUR O'SHAUGHNESSY

REWARD
THE GIFT OF
Imagination

One of the most amazing things about business (and life) is the power of one idea. And one of your great challenges as a leader is to understand how to find and nurture them.

One of the great myths in life is that most breakthrough ideas come from scientists with advanced degrees. While that is true for some industries, most new ideas come from ordinary people with what I'll call "fertile minds"—minds that are always curious and looking for better innovations. "Fertile minds" are not plentiful in most organizations, but they do exist and it is up to the leaders to identify, reward, and cultivate the gift of imagination. For most leaders, however, imagination goes against the grain, because new ideas can rock the boat and cost money. I'd like to share with you some of my favorite examples of the power of one idea.

- Howard Schultz was inspired by a trip to Italy and came back inspired to be the first coffee shop in the United States to focus on, of all things . . . coffee.

- For years, Dunkin Donuts' sales would slow in the summer, until someone thought . . . let's add ice cream. A simple idea that increased sales dramatically.

- McDonald's only served lunch and dinner in all their stores until some maverick franchisee had the courage to ask customers if they'd like to have breakfast at his store. Their answer was yes, and you know the rest of the story.

- Fred Smith, the founder of Federal Express, did a research paper in a business class on the feasibility of starting a "next day delivery business." His professor acknowledged his "off the wall notion" with great skepticism, but with Fred the creative juices had begun to flow.

- In 1951, Kemmons Wilson took his wife and five kids on vacation. He was so frustrated by the second–rate accommodations available for families that he decided to open his own hotel that was clean and never charged extra for children. Plenty of doubters predicted failure because there was nothing like it at the time. He decided to call it "Holiday Inn," and by 1979 he had the largest hotel chain in the world with 1,759 hotels in more than fifty countries, and sales of over $1 billion.

I remember it like it was yesterday. In 1985, we had a small publishing company selling quotation gift books. I had always liked quotes and the books

were selling well. However, one night after work, I was talking with friends, and out of the blue the thought occurred to me: "people really like quotes, wonder if they'd want it to put them on their walls?' From that Successories was born.

This simple concept not only applies to business leaders, it applies to leaders in all areas. For example, Notre Dame's legendary football coach Knute Rockne took his team to a New York stage production for relaxation prior to a big game. While watching the chorus line Rockne conceived the idea of a new offensive formation that gave him a great advantage over his opponents, and eventually revolutionized the game of football.

I could cite hundreds of other examples where one simple idea made a powerful, positive impact. Remember, keep your mind open, and reward the gift of imagination in your organization.

KINDNESS

THE BEST AND MOST BEAUTIFUL
THINGS IN THE WORLD CANNOT
BE SEEN OR TOUCHED.
   THEY MUST BE FELT IN THE HEART.

HELEN KELLER

WALK A MILE IN THEIR *Shoes*

ON MARCH 5, 2003, I turned on *Good Morning, America* while eating breakfast. Charles Gibson was interviewing General Earl Hailston, the commanding general of Marine Forces Central Command. The general was waiting with his troops just a few miles off the border of Iraq . . . waiting to go to war. General Hailston is the only general in the armed forces who had enlisted and came up through the ranks, and as he spoke, I was impressed by his humble and caring attitude.

Toward the end of the interview, his answer to a question touched me deeply. When Charles asked him if he had any hobbies outside his work, the general said, "Yes, I love photography, especially taking photos of my men." He shared that while he had been waiting for the past few days he would take photos of his men, and at night he would email the photos with a brief note to their mothers back in the USA. Charles asked if he could see a sample of a letter, and the general walked into his tent, turned on his computer, and read the last letter he had sent. It said:

Dear Mrs. Johnson,

I thought you might enjoy seeing this picture of your son. He is doing great. I also wanted you to know that you did a wonderful job of raising him. You must be very proud. I can certainly tell you that I'm honored to serve with him in the U.S. Marines.

General Earl Hailston

They don't care how much you know until they know how much you care.

Wow! I had goose bumps as I watched. I then watched Charles randomly interview a few of General Hailston's men. You could feel the genuine love and respect that every one of them had for their leader. You may have heard the quote . . . "They don't care how much you know until they know how much you care." Well, here's a man who truly understood what caring leadership is all about.

GOALS

DREAM BIG DREAMS, BUT
NEVER FORGET THAT
REALISTIC SHORT—TERM
GOALS ARE THE KEYS TO
YOUR SUCCESS.

MAC ANDERSON

Take the INCH BY INCH APPROACH

Patience is bitter, but the fruit is sweet.

WHEN I WAS A FRESHMAN in college, I heard something I never forgot. It was one of the times when I had a lot to do and very little time to do it. I panicked. I was overwhelmed. As I was sitting in my dorm feeling sorry for myself, my roommate came in and said, "Mac, let me share something my grandmother told me a few years ago." She said, "Inch by inch life's a cinch, yard by yard life is hard." Those twelve little words inspired me then and still inspire me today.

Entrepreneurs are not known for their patience. I'm no exception to that rule. But as I've grown older, I've grown wiser, and patience is a virtue I'm beginning to learn. However, hundreds of times in my career I have repeated the words of my roommate's grandmother to get me through tough spots in both my business and personal life. Until recently I thought I was the only one who cherished the inch by inch philosophy, but then I heard an interview with Howard Kruse, the CEO of Blue Bell Creameries, a $400 million ice cream company headquartered in Brenham, Texas. Kruse said, "Our success can be summed up in six words, 'it's a cinch by the inch'." I smiled. You see, the Blue Bell brand is only offered in a handful of states; however, in those places Blue Bell dominates the ice cream market. Outside of these states, if you want a Blue Bell fix you fork over $89 to have four half gallons packed in dry ice and shipped to you. Blue Bell, of course, gets hundreds of offers every year to expand its distribution into other markets, but Howard Kruse says, "We're pretty happy going at our own pace." And once again he smiles and says, "Remember, it's a cinch by the inch."

As leaders, we sometimes start off "half–cocked" and shoot ourselves in the foot. I know . . . I've done it. I've learned that to grow a business profitably, the infrastructure, the system, and the talent to execute the plan all need to be in place. I've also learned that with patience and using the inch by inch approach, business can be less stressful, more profitable, and more fun.

FOCUS ON THE CRITICAL FEW,
NOT THE INSIGNIFICANT MANY.

FOCUS

Focus on Your PRIORITIES

THIS LEADERSHIP LAW is critical to your success in business . . . and also in life. I must admit, however, that this is something that took me a while to learn, and I have a few "battle scars" to show what happens to slow learners regarding this issue. "More is better" sounds reasonable, but I've learned the opposite is usually true. Less, I've discovered, is usually more. The reason, of course, is that there is something powerful about laser-like focus. Having a simple, clearly defined goal can capture the imagination and enthusiasm of your people. It can cut through the night like a beacon. It can bring an idea to life.

In 1985, Jan Carlson had just been named the CEO of Scandinavian Airlines. His company was in trouble. They had just been ranked by a consumer poll as the worst airline in the world. Last in service, last in dependability, and last in profits as a percentage of sales. Yet one year later, in the same poll, they were ranked number one in all three categories. What happened?

Carlson had decided to focus on what he thought was the most critical issue . . . serving the customer. He wanted to keep it simple:

identify every contact between the customer and the employee and treat that contact as "a moment of truth." He set out to let his people know the importance of that moment . . . the captain, the ticket agent, the baggage handler, the flight attendant. "Every moment, every contact" he said, "must be as pleasant,

and as memorable as possible." He figured that he had approximately ten million customers each year, and on average each customer made contact with five of his people for approximately fifteen seconds apiece. Therefore, in his mind, these fifty million contacts, fifteen seconds at a time, would determine the fate of his company.

He set out to share his vision with his twenty thousand employees. He knew the key was to empower the front line. Let them make the decisions and take action, because they were Scandinavian Airlines during those fifteen seconds. He now had twenty thousand people who were energized and ready to go because they were focused on one very important thing . . . making very moment count.

IN THE RACE FOR
QUALITY THERE IS
NO FINISH LINE.

MAKE YOUR BRAND STAND FOR *Something*

"QUALITY IS THE MOTHER . . . and we don't mess with Mom." We embraced this motto early on at Successories, and I was greatly influenced by my creative partner and friend Michael McKee. Our paper stock, our color separations, our frames, and even our shipping cartons were of the highest quality.

Making quality a priority was the most important decision I made in building the Successories brand. In fact, a few years ago in a focus group, twenty customers were asked this question: "If you could write down one word to describe your opinion of Successories, what would the word be?" My heart swelled with pride when eighty percent of the people in the room wrote the word "Quality." Mom was alive and well!

I recall an incident in the late 1980s when we were about $5 million in sales. Cash was tight and we were watching every penny. Mike brought a copy of a new print into my office. It had just come off the press. As we were congratulating one another, my assistant walked in and pointed out that we had misplaced an apostrophe in the quote at the bottom of the page. It should have come before the "S," instead of behind the "S." Michael and I sat there stunned, because to reprint it would cost approximately $5,000, which we didn't have at the time. Although we both knew that very few people would notice, our commitment to quality gave us only one choice . . . destroy the old prints and start over. It was a gut-wrenching decision given our financial situation, but it was the right one. Needless to say, it taught us a valuable lesson in "doing it right the first time."

In 2002, I met Michael McMillan for the first time. He, in my opinion, is one of the best graphic designers in the country. Over lunch, he shared a story of his first encounter with Successories. It happened in 1995 while he was visiting a printer in Minneapolis to discuss the possibility of their printing his coffee table book on Michael Jordan, *Rare Air*. During the tour, he noticed two men with white gloves carefully looking at each print on a stack. Michael said he asked his host, "What's going on over there?" The printer proudly said, "That's work we do for Successories. They insist that every print be hand-inspected and checked for any flaws before we ship them. . . . We give them the 'white glove treatment'." Michael said he never forgot that moment, and afterwards had a much greater respect for our work.

One of my favorite quotes by Will Foster is, "Quality is never an accident . . . It is always the result of high intention, sincere effort, intelligent direction, and skillful execution. It represents the wise choice of many alternatives."

OPTIMISM IS THE FAITH THAT LEADS
TO ACHIEVEMENT

HELEN KELLER

OPTIMISM

Embrace HUMOR, HOPE & OPTIMISM

LAST SUMMER I listened to Democrats, Republicans, prime ministers, kings, and everyday people express their love and admiration for Ronald Reagan. At 93, Reagan died from Alzheimer's Disease. What was it about our fortieth president that so stirred our emotions, that made him a great leader? President George W. Bush, I think, said it best: "Ronald Reagan had the confidence that comes with conviction, the strength that comes with character, the grace that comes with humility, and the humor that comes with wisdom." One headline repeated what I had heard time and time again . . . "The Sun Sets On The Life Of The 'Great Communicator'" In short, Reagan kept it real, he kept simple, and he kept it humorous.

Faith is the strength by which a shattered world shall emerge in light.

More than any leader I've ever seen, Reagan realized the awesome power of communicating with humor. He realized that laughter creates a bond between people like nothing else. He also realized that laughter, especially poking fun at yourself, could defuse almost any issue. A great example of this is that in his first campaign debate against Walter Mondale, Reagan raised concerns about his age, 70, when he gave a confused, uninformed performance. However, at the next debate he defused the issue with humor. He looked right at the audience and said, "I will not make age an issue of this campaign. I am not going to exploit, for political purposes, my opponent's youth and inexperience." The crowd roared with laughter, and the age issue was hardly mentioned again in the campaign.

Even in the assassination attempt on his life, he used humor to put the nation at ease. It was reported that when he first saw his wife, Nancy, at the hospital, he looked up with a smile and said, "Honey, I forgot to duck." Also, as the doctors approached the operating table, he looked at one of his Cabinet members who was at his side and said with a smile . . . "I hope he's a Republican."

Ronald Reagan also understood the power of hope. As a leader, he'll be remembered for many reasons, but perhaps his greatest accomplishment was that he helped to restore our belief in the American Dream. He found no use for doom and gloom in his speeches. His optimism and love of country were contagious, and he always spread hope for a better tomorrow. Even in his last letter to the American people, disclosing that he had Alzheimer's Disease, he still struck a positive note. In his own handwriting he noted, "I now begin the journey that will lead me into the sunset of my life. I know that for America there will always be a bright dawn ahead."

As a leader, you must never, ever, underestimate the power of hope. Without it, you and your team will fail. Helen Keller said, "Optimism is the faith that leads to achievement. Nothing can be done without hope." As the founder of Successories, I occasionally get teased about the positive nature of our products. Some cynics have said they're not in keeping with the real world. It's true, we live in a very negative world, but I choose to reinforce what is positive. I'm very proud of what Successories stands for, and fortunately, we have many customers who agree.

FEELINGS

YOU MAY NOT REMEMBER
WHAT SOMEONE SAYS OR
DOES, BUT YOU'LL NEVER
FORGET ABOUT HOW THEY
MADE YOU FEEL.

Understand
THE 'SOFT STUFF'

HERE'S A SECRET that gives a competitive edge to any leader who really understands it: "The really hard stuff is the soft stuff . . . it's building a culture around the feelings of your customers and your employees." I heard that for the first time a few years ago listening to Tom Asacker speak about building a brand. For me it was one of these "aha" moments that helped put into focus the power of emotions when it comes to our behavior. I heard another memorable quote along those lines not long ago: "You may not remember what someone says or does, but you'll never forget about how they made you feel." This fits well with Asacker's observation that often the customer doesn't really care about you or your company, but they do care about how your products and services make them feel about themselves and the decisions they make.

Mary Kay Ash, the founder of Mary Kay Cosmetics, built her highly successful company around this essential concept—the power of recognition and "feelings." She said two things are more powerful than money and sex, and those are . . . recognition and praise. Even after she became successful, when she would walk into a room she would pretend that everyone in the room had a sign around their neck that said, "Make me feel important." We all want to feel important. No exceptions!

So as a leader, do you truly understand that the really hard stuff is the soft stuff? Are you building your culture around the feelings of your customers and employees? Are you doing everything that you can to make them feel important?

There are two things more powerful than money and sex . . . recognition and praise.

MARY KAY ASH

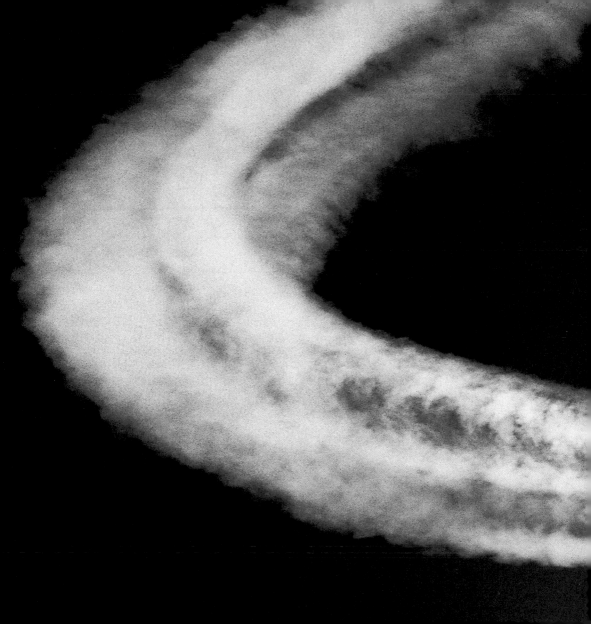

EXCELLENCE

EXCELLENCE IS NOT AN ACT . . .
IT'S A HABIT.

ARISTOTLE

MAKE GOOD *Habits*

ALL OF THE GREAT COACHES I've read about or seen interviewed share a common belief . . . If you make good habits, good habits will make you. This wisdom has been around since ancient times. In fact, one of the best–known quotes from Aristotle is, "Excellence is not an act … it's a habit."

Here's a little test to display the power of our habits. Cross your arms as you normally would, and look down to see which one is on top. When I do this exercise with audiences, invariably about half of the audience members will have their right arm on top (I do) and the other half will have their left on top. When you crossed your arms for the very first time, you might have been still in your playpen, and you've been crossing your arms the same way ever since. Now, cross your arms again, but this time put the wrong arm on top. It feels extremely weird! If I were to challenge you to cross your arms the "wrong" way for the rest of your life, could you do it? Probably. Would it be difficult? You bet it would!

Here's the point: Habits—good, bad, or neutral—are difficult to break. Therefore, the challenge for every leader is to determine the good habits that will drive the success of their organization. Once the desired habits are identified, good training and continual reinforcement are critical in making them part of your organization's culture.

Food for Thought . . .

I am your constant companion.

I am your greatest asset or heaviest burden.

I will push you up to success or down to disappointment.

I am at your command.

Half the things you do might just as well be turned over to me,

For I can do them quickly, correctly, and profitably.

I am easily managed; just be firm with me.

Those who are great, I have made great.

Those who are failures, I have made failures.

I am not a machine, though I work with the precision of a

machine and the intelligence of a person.

You can run me for profit, or you can run me for ruin.

Show me how you want it done. Educate me. Train me.

Lead me. Reward me.

And I will then . . . do it automatically.

I am your servant.

Who am I?

I am a habit.

Nothing is stronger than habit.

OVID

GO OVER,
GO UNDER,
GO AROUND,
OR GO THROUGH,
BUT NEVER GIVE UP.

PERSEVERANCE

Develop a 'REFUSE TO LOSE' ATTITUDE

Like great athletes, most great leaders are very competitive people. They don't like to lose. This attitude can make the difference between success and failure during difficult times.

• Ray Kroc, at 51, tried for two years and talked to more than one hundred people trying to raise the money to start McDonald's.

• Walt Disney failed miserably in his first four attempts to live his dream.

• Henry Ford went bankrupt seven times while trying to launch Ford Motor Company.

Of all the leaders I have worked with, my friend Richard Kent has been the most tenacious, persistent, "refuse to lose" person I have ever known. In 1972, he recruited me to come on as vice president of sales for Orval Kent Foods, a manufacturer of prepared salads sold to restaurants and delicatessens. Richard and I had met in college, and he was convinced that I was the right guy for the job. I was convinced otherwise. For one thing, I had no desire to move to Chicago from my home in Kentucky, and secondly, I knew absolutely nothing about the salad business. After a few conversations on the phone, to which I said "no thanks" as politely as I knew how, Richard took another approach. He said, "Look, you're single. Why don't you just fly up to Chicago for a fun weekend. Everything's on me, no strings attached." It was an offer I couldn't refuse.

I enjoyed my Chicago visit, and while taking me back to the airport, Richard made one last sales pitch. He told me what a great opportunity it would be to grow the company together and to become the leader in a fragmented industry. His passion was contagious. Then he sweetened the pot by offering me ten percent of the company, and if after one year I didn't like it, he'd buy my stock back for a significant amount of money. As I was about to board the plane he said something I never forgot, he said, "Mac, I'm sure there are better people out there to help me grow this company; I just haven't met them yet." He was persistent, he was passionate, he refused to lose. My six years at

Orval Kent were great years. We took the company from $2 million to $15 million, and I got my "Ph.D." in entrepreneurship in those six years. Almost everything that could have happened did, and Richard's passion and survival instincts led us through when times got tough.

I left Orval Kent in 1978 to start McCord Travel, but Richard and I have remained friends over the years. Orval Kent, as he had predicted, did become the country's largest manufacturer of prepared salads with approximately $200 million in sales. As in most companies, there were a few "near death" experiences along the way, but they were conquered by his "refuse to lose" attitude.

Press on: nothing in the world can take the place of perseverance. Talent will not; nothing is more common than unsuccessful men with talent. Genius will not; unrewarded genius is almost a proverb. Education will not; the world is full of educated derelicts. Persistence and determination alone are omnipotent.

CALVIN COOLIDGE

HEARTPOWER

IF YOU THROW YOUR HEART OVER THE FENCE, THE REST WILL FOLLOW

Aim
FOR THE HEART

VINCE LOMBARDI, in his last speech before he died, was addressing a large corporate audience. He said, "I'm going to share with you the key to success in any business." You could have heard a pin drop as they sat on the edges of their seats waiting for the answer. He said, "The secret, in a word, is . . . *heartpower*. Capture the heart, you've captured the person. . . . Get people to fall in love with your company."

This is a very simple, powerful concept. But how does a leader do it? In my opinion, it starts and ends with caring about your people, not as employees, but as human beings.

One of the keys to building heartpower is establishing trust as the cornerstone of your relationships. Trust grows from past actions and is aligned with honesty (telling the truth) and integrity (doing what you say you'll do). Trust, of course, doesn't come quickly. It is earned over a long period of time. I once heard that gaining someone's trust was like filling a bucket one drop at a time. It takes a long time to fill it, but with one swift kick you can lose it all.

Another key to heartpower is respecting others' viewpoints, particularly through the art of listening. This is the most underestimated quality of a great leader. As I mentioned in *The Power of Attitude,* my favorite definition of listening is, "Listening is wanting to hear." It's an emotional process, not just a physical act.

Doing simple, unexpected acts of kindness is the third key to heartpower in any organization. This honors human dignity and radiates compassion and respect. Some ideas appropriate for the workplace include:

Listening is wanting to hear.
JIM CATHCART

- A heartfelt verbal "thank you" or congratulations.

- An unexpected voicemail or email to show appreciation.

- A handwritten note, birthday card, or birthday message.

- A single rose on the desk of someone who went "above and beyond."

- "MAY I HELP?" are the three most appreciated words in the English language. Use them often.

RISK

DON'T BE AFRAID TO GO OUT ON A LIMB . . .
THAT'S WHERE THE FRUIT IS.

Think CHANGE

Consider this. A hundred years ago . . .

- There were only 8,000 cars in the United States and 144 miles of paved road.

- The average U.S. worker made between $200 and $400 a year.

- Only 8 percent of homes had a telephone.

- Alabama, Mississippi, Iowa, and Tennessee were all more populated than California.

- Only 6 percent of Americans had graduated from high school.

We must never forget . . . Change is inevitable, but growth is optional.

Of all U.S. companies, 3M is probably the most famous in creating a culture of innovation, or "disciplined creativity," as some call it. This didn't happen by accident. In 1929, founder William McKnight turned innovation into a systematic, reputable process. He rewarded the lone spirits within the company who were "given permission" to fight for their new ideas. The innovative creative culture has fueled many success stories along the way, including the development of Post–it® Notes. Although Post–its failed their initial market test, the 3M scientist who invented the product hooked a core group of users by distributing free samples to the staff at headquarters in Minneapolis. He was allowed to fight for his product's success, and the rest, as they say, is history.

How can you, as a leader, put your company in a position to exploit change? It's not easy. According to Peter Drucker, most companies find it less difficult to come up with new ideas than to let go of old ones. I certainly agree with him that most leaders are too busy solving today's problems to focus on tomorrow's opportunities. It's human nature. To put innovation on the "front burner," Drucker recommends that your monthly operating report have two pages: one listing the problems and one targeting "possible opportunities." This, he says, will force each leader to keep innovation and continuous improvement front and center. In fact, Drucker recommends that every three years each product, process, and distribution channel should be put on trial for its life.

Over the past fifteen years, Successories has been known as a creative company. We invented our niche of combining photographs with words to reinforce core values, and we moved quickly to grow it.

One thing is certain: innovation starts with creative people who are allowed to take risks and be rewarded for their efforts.

AUTHENTICITY

INTEGRITY DOES NOT BLOW IN THE WIND OR CHANGE WITH THE TIDE. IT IS THE INNER IMAGE OF OUR TRUE SELVES.

Strive for AUTHENTICITY

BILL GEORGE was the CEO and the innovator–in–chief who transformed Minneapolis–based Medtronics Info into the world's largest medical device manufacturer. Since George left Medtronics in 2002, he has been speaking and writing on what he thinks is the missing ingredient for many of today's leaders. His answer is authentic leadership—that is, business leaders who demonstrate integrity, values, and conviction. Leaders who have the courage to put customers and employees before Wall Street, who speak out to right a wrong and admit their mistakes. I could not agree more.

I recently read his bestselling book, *Authentic Leadership . . . Discovering the Secrets to Creating Lasting Value,* and it's one of the best books by a business leader I've ever read.

One of the chapters in George's book is titled "Values Don't Lie". In it he says that one of the greatest challenges in business today is to create a culture that is both values–centered and performance–driven. "Values," he says, "begin with telling the truth internally and externally. Integrity must run deep in the fabric of an organization's culture. It guides the everyday actions of employees and is central to its business conduct."

Another thing to remember about authentic leaders is this; they don't expect respect . . . they earn it. Jeff King is a sled dog racer who has won the 1,000–mile Iditarod Race from Anchorage to Nome, Alaska, three times (1993, 1996, and 1998). Jeff said that when he starts the race, he starts with sixteen dogs and rotates the lead dog frequently to  give all the dogs a chance to lead. Eventually, he finds the dog with the most energy, enthusiasm, and persistence, and that dog becomes the leader of the pack. In 1998 the lead dog was a 2–year–old female named Jenna. This was unusual because there were only two females in the pack and she was younger and smaller than all the male dogs. But Jeff said she was the leader. "When a blizzard came she didn't give up. She kept barking and running even when the snow was over her head, and inspired us all to keep going." In short, Jenna earned the right to lead.

George Washington was not always a great tactician, but all historians agree . . . he was a great general. Why? His soldiers loved and respected him. He lived with them. When they were cold he shivered with them; when there was not enough food to go around, he did without. He knew that to win the revolution he must first win the hearts of his soldiers. His self–sacrifice and concern for them as human beings made Washington one of the greatest generals in history.

ATTITUDE

ATTITUDE IS A LITTLE
THING THAT MAKES A
BIG DIFFERENCE.

Hire GREAT PEOPLE

I'M A BIG FAN of Nordstrom's, and my wife is a bigger fan. Recently, I had the opportunity to have lunch with a Nordstrom's executive and shared some of the great service moments his company had provided to the Anderson family. Then I asked the all–important question, "What is the key to Nordstrom's success?" He answered as follows: "We hire great people and empower them to do whatever it takes to satisfy the customer." Then he continued, "We learned a long time ago that you can't send a duck to eagle school."

I said, "Excuse me?"

He elaborated: "You can't send a duck to eagle school. You can't teach someone to

want to serve, you can't teach a smile, you can't teach personality. However, you can hire people who have those qualities, and we can teach them our products and teach them our culture."

As leaders, how many of us are guilty of hiring ducks, thinking they could become eagles? I would be the first to raise my hand and admit it. What has happened, at least with me, is that I needed people quickly, and even knowing they weren't exactly what I was looking for, I rationalized ("with a little work this duck could be an eagle") and hired them anyway. This can be, and usually is, one of the most expensive mistakes any leader can make. You must constantly remind yourself that hiring the right person for your team is your most important job as a manager. With each hire, your credibility and your team's success are on the line.

*Ability is what you're capable of
doing. Motivation determines
what you do. Attitude determines
how well you do it.*

LOU HOLTZ

THINGS THAT MATTER MOST

MUST NEVER BE AT THE MERCY

OF THINGS THAT MATTER LEAST

GOETHE

VALUES

Reinforce CORE VALUES

IF I WERE TO POLL a hundred leaders and ask the question, "Is it important to reinforce core values" . . . all would probably say, "Yes!" However, this is one of the areas where there's usually a big gap between "I should" and "I did." It sounds like the right thing to do, but rarely is there a plan to make it happen.

In a perfect world, we hear something once, record it in our brain, and never need to hear it again. But in a world where our brains are being bombarded from all directions, continual reinforcement is needed to cut through the clutter and make it a part of your organization's culture. In fact, the need to reinforce core values was my inspiration to launch Simple Truths, a gift book publishing company to allow organizations to share their core values with their employees and their customers. It was my belief that small books (less can be more) beautifully designed, with excellent content are what people will read and remember. Thus our name . . . Simple Truths.

Paul Adams is one leader who truly understands the importance of core values and the need to reinforce them. His life is devoted to running Providence St. Mel, a private school in one of the poorest neighborhoods in Chicago. Under Paul's leadership 100 percent of the students attending Providence St. Mel go on to universities, many to some of the top schools in the country.

The culture of this wonderful school is reflected in a mission statement, or pledge, that the students recite in unison every morning:

At Providence St. Mel, we believe . . .

We believe in the creation of inspired lives
produced by the miracle of hard work. We are
not frightened by the challenges of reality,
but believe that we can change our conception
of the world and our place within it.
So, we work, plan, build, and dream, in that order.

We believe that one must earn the right to dream.

Our talent, discipline and integrity will be our contribution to a new world.

Because we believe that we can take this place,

this time, and this people, and make a better place,

A better time and a better people.

With God's help, we will either find a way, or make one.

Paul Adams is a great leader, and a hero in the eyes of many. He also understands that continual reinforcement is critical to keeping goals and values in focus.

DISCOVERY

LEADERS ARE LIKE
EAGLES. THEY DON'T
FLOCK, YOU FIND THEM
ONE AT A TIME.

EXPECT THE *Unexpected*

ONE OF THE MOST fascinating things about leadership is that sometimes a person you least expect will step up and emerge as a leader. It can happen at any time, but it has been my experience that any emerging leader possesses two key traits . . . attitude and heart.

I recently developed a friendship with speaker and author Barbara Glanz, and she told me a wonderful story about an unexpected leader.

A few years ago, she spoke to employees from a supermarket chain. About three weeks later she got a phone call from a person who said his name was Johnny and that he was a bagger in the store. He also told her that he had Down syndrome. Johnnny then told Barbara how much he liked what she said about serving the customer. That night, he and his father had set up a document on the computer where every night he would type a thought for the day that he found. He then printed them, cut them out, and signed his name on the back of each slip of paper. The next day as he bagged groceries, he tucked the encouraging thought into each person's grocery bag.

One month later the manager called Barbara and said, "You won't believe what happened today! The line at Johnny's checkout was three times longer than any other line. I called for more cashiers to the front, but the customers said, "No, we want to be in Johnny's lane. We want his thought for the day."

The manager said Johnny had become the most important person in the store!

Three months later, the store manager called Barbara again and said: "You and Johnny have transformed our store! Now, in the floral department when they have a broken flower or an unused corsage, they will go out on the floor and find an elderly woman or a little girl and pin it on them. One of our meat packers loves Snoopy, so he bought Snoopy stickers for each package. Thanks to Johnny's example, we're having fun and so are our customers!"

This story shows how one person, by setting an example, can emerge as a leader in any organization. It starts with a willing heart, a positive attitude, and a desire to make a difference.

Note: I'm pleased to say that Johnny's story has inspired a gift book with Barbara, Ken Blanchard, and me, titled *The Simple Truths of Service*.

Great leadership usually starts with a willing heart, a positive attitude, and a desire to make a difference.

MAC ANDERSON

TRUST

TRUST, NOT TECHNOLOGY, IS
THE ISSUE OF THE DECADE

TOM PETERS

Create AN ATTITUDE OF Ownership

In order that people may be happy in their work, these three things are needed: They must be fit for it. They must not do too much of it. And they must have a sense of success in it.

JOHN RUSKIN

Mary, a housekeeper at the Four Seasons in Austin, Texas, clearly sees herself as a one–woman business enterprise. She "owns" her floor. "These are my rooms, she says, "and I have to take care of my" customers. I don't need permission to do what's right. I just do it."

This attitude of "ownership" is the result of entrepreneurial thinking that is discussed in the book *Motivating Employees* by Anne Bruce and James Pepitone. Quite simply, workers feel appreciated when they are empowered with responsibility. As a manager, by giving away your power, you allow your employees to share your responsibility and authority. Your job is to remove the obstacles. You give them the tools, the information, and the training they need to succeed.

Trust, however, is key to managing people and building a high performance company. It is the foundation on which relationships are built. According to Tom Peters,

"Technique and technology are important. But adding trust is the issue of the decade." Peters suggest that managers must take a "high–tech and high–trust" approach, putting the issue of trust at the top of the agenda and treating it like "a hard issue, not a soft issue." If employees feel you don't trust them to their jobs correctly and well, they'll be reluctant to do much without your approval. On the other hand, when they feel trusted, that you believe they'll do the right things well, they'll naturally want to do things well and be deserving of your trust.

To create an environment that embraces entrepreneurial thinking, consider these three keys:

1. Explain the company's mission, its goals and most importantly, its strategies to achieve those goals. If employees understand the big picture, they are much more likely to understand their roles and why the company values your contributions.

2. Help your employees understand the competition. Appealing to their competitive nature and their pride can generate excellent results.

3. Encourage risk–taking and innovative thinking. This one can be scary to many leaders, but great leaders realize that long–term survival depends on taking risks.

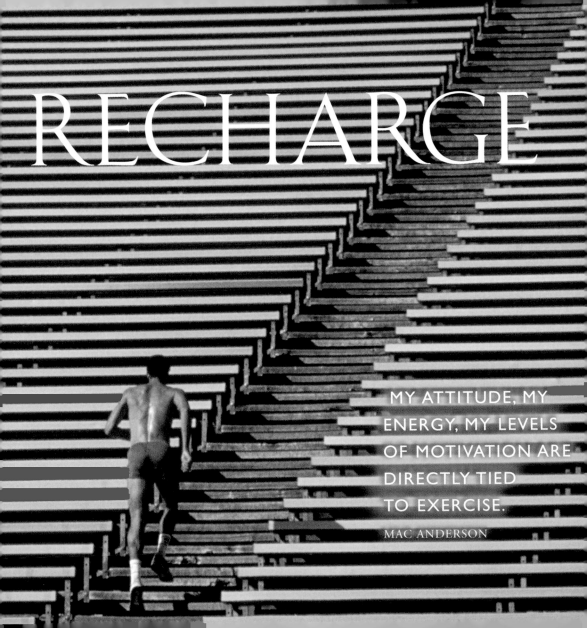

RECHARGE

MY ATTITUDE, MY
ENERGY, MY LEVELS
OF MOTIVATION ARE
DIRECTLY TIED
TO EXERCISE.

MAC ANDERSON

MANAGE YOUR *Energy*

NOT LONG AGO, I had the opportunity to spend some time with bestselling author John Maxwell. The conversation turned to how managing your energy can be one of the keys to leadership. Leadership and energy are joined at the hip. It is impossible to have one without the other. According to John, it all starts with knowing yourself, knowing your limitations, and knowing when you perform best. The key, for him, is to schedule his most crucial activities when his energy levels at their peak. John, for example, schedules his important meetings and his writing time in the mornings when he feels the most energized. Activities of less urgency are scheduled in the afternoons. Also, as he winds down at home in the evenings, he saves an hour or two for writing letters and for light reading. Of course, he said, a schedule doesn't always cooperate, but following this general philosophy has served him well.

Speaker and author Jim Cathcart says that to be at your best, find your zone of optimum velocity by observing the pace and intensity at which you perform best. This is the zone at which you are most creative, unstressed, happy and productive.

Above the zone: First you experience stress and frustration, then anxiety, and finally burnout. At this level you are overwhelming yourself with too much to accomplish at one time. Lighten up a bit to get back on track.

In the zone: You are at your best. Not stressed, going with the flow of work naturally, productive and self–assured, challenged but not overwhelmed, motivated and able to roll with problems.

Below the zone: first you experience boredom, then apathy, and finally depression. You feel useless and artificial; self–esteem suffers. Bite off more and take on a greater challenge to get back on track.

For me the key to managing my energy is exercise. It almost sounds too simple to be important, however, without exercise my energy levels and my attitude "take a hit."

Lastly, protecting and replenishing your emotional energy is critical for every leader. Mira Kirshenbaum in her book *The Emotional Energy Factor* offers a refreshing, down–to–earth approach:

"First, you plug the leaks: learn to recognize what drains your energy—life situations, toxic people, or habits such as worry, indecision or guilt. Second, you identify what fills your tank—pleasure, prayer, anticipation, or fun—and give yourself more."

Always laugh when you can.
It is cheap medicine.

LORD BYRON

PRIORITIES

A HUNDRED YEARS FROM NOW IT WILL NOT MATTER WHAT YOUR BANK ACCOUNT WAS, THE SORT OF HOUSE YOU LIVED IN, OR THE KIND OF CAR YOU DROVE. BUT THE WORLD MAY BE DIFFERENT BECAUSE YOU WERE IMPORTANT IN THE LIFE OF A CHILD.

THE *Most* IMPORTANT LEADER

THE TITLE BESTOWED on the most important leader in the world today is not president, queen, or prime minister. It is parent. What the present generation of parents teaches today will set the stage for our tomorrows. For . . . "our children are the living messages we send to a time we will not see."

I recently had the opportunity to co–author (with Lance Wubbels) a beautiful gift book titled *To A Child . . . Love Is Spelled T.I.M.E.* Part of my passion for this project was based on the fact that as a father I made mistakes, and it was my hope that this book would remind parents of the importance of TIME with their children. Lance wrote this passage and it's one of my favorite parts of the book:

> Time is the raw material of your relationship with your child and must be guarded at all costs. It's true what they say: a bucket with a hole in it gets just as empty as a bucket that is deliberately kicked over. Life will shout a thousand demands to take you away from time spent with your child. If you permit the urgent to rule, you will lose time you can never recover or catch with your hand. What happens in the changing life of your child today will never be repeated. All the gold in the world cannot buy back either the little delights of the day or the big pleasures that happen without announcement or a plan. You simply have to be there.

As a parent, you are the leader for your child, and your every action is being watched. This is the most important job you'll ever have. The quote on a print we have at Successories says it best:

"A hundred years from now, it will not matter what your bank account was, the sort of house you lived in, or the kind of car you drove. But the world may be different because you were important in the life of a child."

Someone sent me a beautiful poem the other day titled "Little Eyes Upon You." I don't know who wrote it, but I'll share the last verse with you:

There's a wide—eyed little boy
Who believes you're always right.
And his eyes are always open
While he watches day and night.
You are setting an example.
Every day, in all you do.
For the little boy who's waiting
To grow up and be like you.

Never forget . . . "To the world you may be just one person . . . but to one person you might just be the world"

CULTIVATE

PULL THE WEEDS.
OTHERWISE THE TEAM,
JUST LIKE THE GARDEN,
CANNOT GROW.

JOHN MURPHY

PULL THE *Weeds*

If it weren't for people, leadership would be easy.

AS A LEADER, it is one thing to be loyal; it's another to be dumb. Looking back at my career as an entrepreneur, there were a number of times when I was loyal to a fault. ("Dumb" is a harsh word, but probably fitting.) My instincts were telling me that a person was not right for the job, but my heart kept telling me to give them more time. Throughout my thirty years in business, whenever I began to lose confidence in any employee the situation never got better by waiting. I've learned that is better to hire slowly to make sure you get the right person and to fire quickly when your gut says you made a mistake. Or as John Murphy says in his book *Pulling Together,* "Pull the weeds." Murphy says: "Life is full of choices. Some people will choose to work with the team and embrace your corporate culture. Others will not."

As leaders we must continually pull the weeds; otherwise the team cannot grow. A weed is someone who makes their own rules undermining team consensus, someone who refuses to share and participate, someone who rejects accountability and shifts blame to others. Don't be fooled. Weeds may seem harmless . . . but they can't be trusted. They're doing everything they can to take over your garden.

For years, Jack Welch, retired CEO for General Electric, had a rule that his managers must develop criteria to measure the performance of all employees. They were instructed to identify the bottom ten percent in each department and replace them with "new blood." Although this controversial rule eventually was eliminated and caused some problems for G.E., it's hard to argue with the long–term success of the company. I strongly disagree with tying employment to a percentage, but I do know that new people and fresh ideas can be good for any company, especially if they are replacing negative non–performers.

In the long run, if a leader continues to take the path of least resistance and doesn't pull an obvious "weed," he or she will risk losing credibility with those who are performing well.

SUCCESS

TRY NOT TO BECOME A PERSON OF SUCCESS,
BUT RATHER TRY TO BECOME A PERSON OF VALUE.

ALBERT EINSTEIN

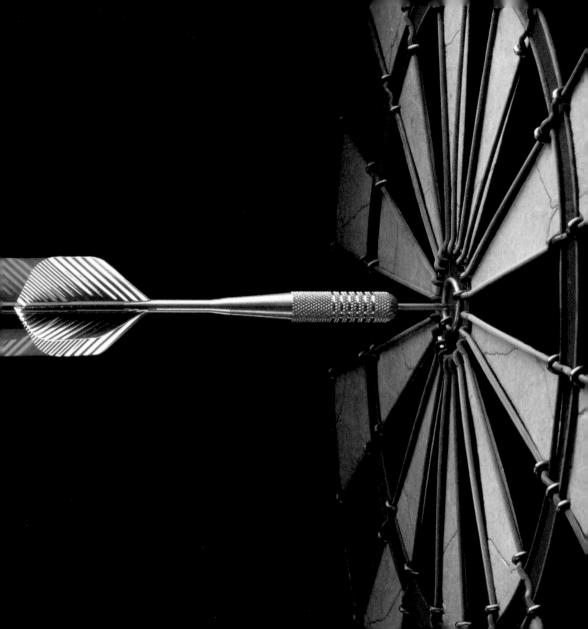

LEAD WITH *Values*

WHEN IT COMES to organizational values your job, as a leader, is critical. First you must make sure everyone understands the values, and secondly, you must guide your people to practice them. Most importantly, however, you must walk the talk.

In his book *Leading With Values,* Bud Bilanich says, "'Values ground an organization—providing direction for people who find themselves in ambiguous situations. They are guides for decision making. Many leaders fail, however, by opting for values they never really believed. They sound good, but have no heart."

Putting values first doesn't always come easy. Sometimes it takes courage . . . a lot of courage. In l982, James Burke, the CEO at Johnson and Johnson, made a courageous decision to pull Tylenol capsules off the shelves in response to a cyanide-poisoning crisis. He took a $100 million hit to the bottom line.

When he called a meeting with his key executives, he brought a copy of the company Credo written in 1943 by R. W. Johnson, Jr. On the Credo, it clearly spelled out, "We believe our first responsibility is . . . to mothers and fathers and all others who use our products." Burke said, "Here's the Credo. If we're not going to live by it, let's tear it off the wall. If we are, however, we know what we have to do." The team didn't need to debate whether customer safety outweighed short-term financial concerns, because the debating had been done decades earlier.

The alignment with their core values cost the company dearly in financial terms, but the return on the investment came through increased customer confidence and loyalty, boosting the product to an even greater market share than it had had before the crisis.

Never forget, organizational values start and end with you, the leader. Whether your example is good or bad, expect most employees to follow your lead. As Bud Bilanich said, "You need to know the way, show the way, and go the way. By doing this you will have earned the right to insist that others do the same."

THE HEART THAT GIVES, GATHERS

HANNAH MOORE

HUMILITY

Develop a
SERVICE ATTITUDE

THE GREAT LEADERS—whether they're presidents, teachers, coaches, soldiers or CEOs—know they are there not to feed their egos, but to serve others. This humble, caring, service–oriented attitude, more than anything else, fosters admiration and respect among the people being led.

When I think of a service attitude, my good friend Scott Morrison comes to mind. I've known Scott for twenty–five years. We first met when he was president of Arvida Resorts and had bottom–line responsibility for the Boca Raton Hotel and Club, Long Boat Key Club, and several other major resorts. When I lived in Boca Raton, I occasionally would join Scott for lunch at the hotel. It never ceased to amaze me how he treated every employee he met. Although the hotel had more than a thousand employees, as we walked the grounds he greeted almost everyone by name and with a sincere smile and a handshake. Many times he would ask about their families and their jobs, and I could sense the admiration they had for him.

A great poem by Will Allen Dromgoole, "The Bridge Builder," teaches some valuable lessons about having a service attitude.

An old man going down a long highway

Came in the evening cold and gray

To a chasm vast and deep and wide

Through which was flowing a sullen tide.

The old man crossed in the twilight dim;

That swollen stream held no fears for him;

But he turned when safe on the other side

And built a bridge to span the tide.

"Old Man," said a fellow pilgrim near,

"You are wasting your strength with building here;

Your journey will end with the ending day.

You never again must pass this way;

You have crossed the chasm deep and wide—

Why build you this bridge at the eventide?"

The builder lifted his old gray head.

"Good friend, in the path I have come," he said,

"There followeth after me today

A youth whose feet must pass this way.

This swollen stream which was naught to me

To that fair—haired youth may a pitfall be;

He, too, must cross in the twilight dim;

Good friend, I am building the bridge for him."

*The road to service
is traveled with integrity,
compassion, and understanding.*

TAKE ACTION

YOU CANNOT DISCOVER
NEW OCEANS UNLESS YOU
HAVE THE COURAGE TO LOSE
SIGHT OF THE SHORE.

TAKE *Action*

You'll always miss 100% of the shots you don't take.

BOLD IDEAS are worth nothing until a leader has the courage to take action. One of my favorite prints that we created at Successories says, "You cannot discover new oceans unless you have the courage to lose sight of the shore." The only way we can learn and grow is to leave our comfort zone to risk. Along the way, many people told me that Successories wouldn't work and that I was wasting my time trying to build the company. I thought otherwise and was willing to "bet the farm" that I was right.

Throughout history, our leaders understood that the essence of leadership is about taking action. There always comes a point where discussions must end and actions begin, even if no desirable solution has been reached.

Katherine Graham, longtime publisher for the *Washington Post,* was considered one of the great leaders of our time. She took the leadership position of the family company after her husband, Philip, committed suicide. The *Post* was an undistinquished regional paper at the time, and her goal was to create a paper equal to the *New York Times*. In 1971, however, she was confronted with a monumental decision about what to do with the Pentagon Papers, a leaked Defense Department study that revealed government deceptions about the Vietnam War. The *New York Times* had already incurred a court injunction for publishing excerpts, and if she decided to publish, the company could be prosecuted under the Espionage Act. That, in turn, could jeopardize the pending stock offering and their lucrative television licenses. She said in her memoirs, *Personal History,* . . . "I was risking the whole company on this one decision." She decided to publish the papers and said, "Survival at the cost of the company's soul would be worse than not surviving."

Eventually, she was vindicated by the Supreme Court and went on to build a great newspaper and a great company. Courage, it is said, is not the absence of fear but the ability to act in its presence. With courage at her side, Katherine Graham risked everything to follow her convictions.

LEADERSHIP

A LEADER'S JOB IS TO LOOK INTO THE FUTURE AND SEE THE ORGANIZATION, NOT AS IT IS, BUT AS IT SHOULD BE.

YOUR CUSTOMERS MUST COME *Second*

TO BUILD A "customer first" culture, you must put them second. Your people must come first, because there is a rule of thumb in business that says, "Your people will only treat your customers as well as they are being treated; thus to have satisfied customers, they must be served by passionate people."

Howard Schultz, the founder of Starbucks, is one of my favorite leaders. His book *Pour Your Heart Into It* is excellent. In it he offers in great detail all the obstacles he overcame in turning his vision into reality.

Early on, Schultz realized that the key to his success was to recruit well-educated people who were eager to communicate their passion for coffee. This, he felt, would be his competitive advantage in an industry where turnover was 300 percent a year. To hire the best people, he also knew he must be willing to pay them

103

more than the going wage and offer health benefits that weren't available elsewhere. He saw that part-time people made up two-thirds of his employee base, and no one in the restaurant industry offered benefits to part-timers. Schultz went to work in an effort to sell his board of directors to increase expenses while most restaurant executives in the 1980s were looking for ways to cut costs. Initially Schultz's pleas to investors and the board fell on deaf ears because Starbucks was still losing money. But Schultz was persistent. He was looking long term and was committed to growing the business with passionate people. He won, and he said many times afterward that this decision was one of the most important decisions, if not the most important, that he had made at Starbucks. His employee retention rate was about five times the industry average, but more importantly he could attract people with great attitudes who made their customers feel welcome and at home.

Over the years, Schultz often showed how much he cared for his people. Early on July 7,1997, he and his family were asleep at home in East Hampton, New York. The phone rang and he learned that three Starbucks employees had been murdered in a botched robbery in Washington, D.C. A stunned Schultz immediately chartered a plane and arrived there before 9 a.m. that morning. He stayed for a week working with police, meeting with the victim's families, and attending funerals. He ultimately decided that future profits of the store would go to organizations working for violence prevention and victims' rights.

Howard Schultz "gets it." A common quote of the Starbucks team tells it all: "We aren't in the coffee business serving people. We're in the people business serving coffee."

The quality of your people will determine your destiny.

WISDOM IS KNOWING THE

RIGHT PATH TO TAKE.

INTEGRITY IS TAKING IT.

INTEGRITY

LEAD WITH
Integrity

THE PERSON WITH whom you compete the most is the person you see when you look in the mirror.

Todd Duncan observed, "Integrity is not automatic. It results from self-discipline, hard-found character, solidified beliefs, and the relentless pursuit of honesty." What a great quote about the human quality that is most necessary to achieve long-term business success.

James Cash Penney was one of the nation's great retailing pioneers. Born the son of a minister in 1875, he went into the dry-goods business as a salesman. He quickly became a manager and part owner of his own store. Penney was committed to conducting business with integrity. He insisted on selling only quality merchandise, keeping price mark-ups to a minimum, and operating by the Golden Rule. By 1912, Penney owned a chain of thirty-four Golden Rule stores. In 1919, he changed the name to J.C. Penney. By 1928, the chain had grown to more than a thousand stores. In describing the secret to his success, Penney said: "There are no secrets. In retailing, the formula is a basic liking for human beings, plus integrity and hard work."

Colin Powell is regarded as a man of great integrity. In a recent interview, he pointed on his desk to one of his most prized possessions, a photo of Ronald Reagan and Powell. The photo was inscribed by Reagan as follows:

"Colin, when you tell me something I know it is so."

As a leader, you could receive no greater compliment.

I hope I shall possess firmness and virtue enough to maintain what I consider the most enviable of all titles, the character of an honest man.

GEORGE WASHINGTON

PASSION

TO LOVE WHAT YOU DO AND
FEEL THAT IT MATTERS . . .
HOW COULD ANYTHING
BE MORE FUN?

KATHERINE GRAHAM

Love WHAT YOU DO

*Many things will
catch your eye,
but very few will
capture your heart.
Pursue those.*

OF ALL THE QUALITIES a leader can have, passion is the most important. Passion, however, is something you can't fake. It starts in the soul and is fueled by belief that what you're doing is important. At 70, Jane Goodall is still a leader. She is the renowned primatologist who has spent her life working with chimpanzees and creating global awareness for the environment. When you ask her to sum up her reasons for success in her field. She simply says . . . "I love what I do, and it shows." Goodall's passion is reflected in these words: "Every day has to count. Every day, I want to learn something; every day, I want to be inspired; every day, I want to inspire someone."

Katherine Graham, longtime publisher for the *Washington Post,* said this, "To love what you do and feel that it matters . . . how could anything be more fun?"

When I hear the word "passion," Oprah Winfrey immediately comes to mind. Her inspirational story certainly proves that the American Dream is alive and well. When celebrating her 50th birthday, she had this to say:

"I treasure every moment more than ever. I'm ready to claim this next decade for all it's worth and take it to the max. I look to the future with a bursting desire to be more, love and live more preciously."

Oprah Winfrey loves what she does. She lives her dream with passion and has made a positive difference in many lives, not only in this country but around the world.

PURPOSE

LET YOUR LIGHT SO SHINE BEFORE
MEN, THAT THEY MAY SEE YOUR
GOOD WORKS AND GLORIFY
YOUR FATHER IN HEAVEN.

MATTHEW 5:16

MAKE A
Difference

IN THE DEEPEST PART of our souls, most of us want to make a difference with our lives. We want to do something positive that will live on after we're gone. As leaders, we're in a position of influence, and what we say and do will change lives . . . in a positive or negative way.

About a year ago, I had the opportunity to spend couple of days with author Ken Blanchard at his lake home in upstate New York. Our conversation took us down the path of talking about how we could do some things together to make a difference. He then reached over to his briefcase and pulled out his daily journal. He said, "I want to share with you something that I read every

The surest way to happiness is to lose yourself in a cause greater than yourself.

day . . . and every day it continues to inspire me to try to do more with my life." He then read it aloud:

He was born in an obscure village, the child of a peasant woman. He grew up in still another village, where He worked in a carpenter's shop until He was thirty. Then for three years He was an itinerant preacher. He never wrote a book, never held an office, never had a family or owned a house. He never went to college. He never visited a big city. He never traveled two hundred miles from the place where He was born. He did none of the things one usually associates with greatness. He had no credentials but Himself.

He was only thirty–three when the tide of public opinion turned against Him. His friends ran away. He was turned over to his enemies and went through the mockery of a trial. He was nailed to a cross between two thieves. While He was dying His executioners gambled for His clothing, the only property He had on earth. When He was dead He was laid in a borrowed grave through the pity of a friend.

Twenty centuries have come and gone, and today Jesus is the central figure of the human race and the leader of mankind's progress. All the armies that ever marched, all the navies that ever sailed, all the parliaments that ever sat, all the kings that ever reigned put together have not affected the life of mankind on this earth as much as that ONE SOLITARY LIFE.

This powerful, thought-provoking essay titled "One Solitary Life" was written by Dr. James Allen Francis. The words remind us that making a difference with our lives might have nothing to do with education, wealth, power, or fame, but everything to do with love, kindness, compassion, and serving others.

*My personal thanks to four great photographers
whose photos are featured in this book.—Mac*

BRUCE HEINEMANN'S
photos appear on pages 1, 22, 42, 50, 54, 66, 82, 88, 114, back cover
www.theartofnature.com

KEN JENKINS'S photos appear on pages 8, 21, 38, front cover
www.kenjenkins.com

STEVE TERRILL'S photos appear on pages 10, 86, 94
www.terrillphoto.com

JIM BRANDENBURG'S
photos appear on pages 30, 34, 62, 74, 84, and 98
www.jimbrandenburg.com

MAC ANDERSON is the founder of Successories®, Inc., the leader in designing and marketing products for motivation and recognition. Successories, however, is not the first success story for Mac. He was also the founder and CEO of McCord Travel, the largest travel company in the Midwest, and part owner/VP of sales and marketing for Orval Kent Food Company, the country's largest manufacturer of prepared salads. Mac's accomplishments in these three unrelated industries provide some insight into his passion and leadership skills.

Mac brings the same passion to his speaking and writing. He speaks to many corporate audiences on a variety of topics, including leadership, motivation, and team building.

He has written three books, *The Nature of Success, The Power of Attitude,* and *The Essence of Leadership,* and has coauthored *To a Child, Love is Spelled T-I-M-E* and *The Race.* Mac also recently launched Simple Truths, a company publishing corporate gift books to reinforce core values.

For more information, please visit www.simpletruths.com or www.macanderson.com.

THE PRICE OF GREATNESS

IS RESPONSIBILITY

WINSTON CHURCHILL